D0605171

LET'S EXPLORE THE STATES

Lower Atlantic

Florida
Georgia
South Carolina

Daniel E. Harmon

Mason Crest
450 Parkway Drive, Suite D
Broomall, PA 19008
www.masoncrest.com

©2016 by Mason Crest, an imprint of National Highlights, Inc.

Printed and bound in the United States of America.

CPSIA Compliance Information: Batch #LES2015.
For further information, contact Mason Crest at 1-866-MCP-Book.

First printing
1 3 5 7 9 8 6 4 2

Library of Congress Cataloging-in-Publication Data

Harmon, Daniel E.
  Lower Atlantic : Florida, Georgia, South Carolina / Daniel E. Harmon.
    pages cm. — (Let's explore the states)
  Includes bibliographical references and index.
  ISBN 978-1-4222-3325-2 (hc)
  ISBN 978-1-4222-8610-4 (ebook)
  1. Atlantic States—Juvenile literature. 2. Florida—Juvenile literature.
  3. Georgia—Juvenile literature. 4. South Carolina—Juvenile literature. I. Title.
  F106.H236 2015
  975—dc23

                            2014050184

Let's Explore the States series ISBN: 978-1-4222-3319-1

Publisher's Note: Websites listed in this book were active at the time of publication. The publisher is not responsible for websites that have changed their address or discontinued operation since the date of publication. The publisher reviews and updates the websites each time the book is reprinted.

About the Author: Daniel E. Harmon has written more than 90 books, including profiles of U.S. states and international studies. A veteran magazine, newsletter, and newspaper editor and writer, he has contributed thousands of articles to national and regional periodicals. He lives in Spartanburg, South Carolina.

Picture Credits: Library of Congress: 14, 18 (top), 33, 38 (left; bottom right), 53, 54; NASA/Bill Ingalls: 15; National Archives: 31, 38 (top right); National Park Service: 52; used under license from Shutterstock, Inc: 1, 5, 6, 9 (top), 10, 12 (bottom right), 13, 16, 21, 24, 27, 28 (bottom), 30, 35, 39, 40, 41, 44, 45, 47, 48, 49, 56, 57, 58; Songquan Deng / Shutterstock.com: 12 (bottom left); Fotoluminate LLC / Shutterstock.com: 9 (bottom); D. Free / Shutterstock.com: 18 (bottom); Nataliya Hora / Shutterstock.com: 51 (bottom); Jay L. / Shutterstock.com: 28 (top); Sandi Mako / Shutterstock.com: 12 (top right); Meunierd / Shutterstock.com: 12 (top left); Ruth Peterkin / Shutterstock.com: 19; Joseph Sohm / Shutterstock.com: 60; Elvis Vaughn / Shutterstock.com: 51 (top); Katherine Welles / Shutterstock.com: 37.

Table of Contents

KEY ICONS TO LOOK FOR:

Words to Understand: These words with their easy-to-understand definitions will increase the reader's understanding of the text, while building vocabulary skills.

Sidebars: This boxed material within the main text allows readers to build knowledge, gain insights, explore possibilities, and broaden their perspectives by weaving together additional information to provide realistic and holistic perspectives.

Research Projects: Readers are pointed toward areas of further inquiry connected to each chapter. Suggestions are provided for projects that encourage deeper research and analysis.

Text-Dependent Questions: These questions send the reader back to the text for more careful attention to the evidence presented there.

Series Glossary of Key Terms: This back-of-the book glossary contains terminology used throughout this series. Words found here increase the reader's ability to read and comprehend higher-level books and articles in this field.

LET'S EXPLORE THE STATES

Atlantic: North Carolina, Virginia, West Virginia
Central Mississippi River Basin: Arkansas, Iowa, Missouri
East South-Central States: Kentucky, Tennessee
Eastern Great Lakes: Indiana, Michigan, Ohio
Gulf States: Alabama, Louisiana, Mississippi
Lower Atlantic: Florida, Georgia, South Carolina
Lower Plains: Kansas, Nebraska
Mid-Atlantic: Delaware, District of Columbia, Maryland
Non-Continental: Alaska, Hawaii
Northern New England: Maine, New Hampshire, Vermont
Northeast: New Jersey, New York, Pennsylvania
Northwest: Idaho, Oregon, Washington
Rocky Mountain: Colorado, Utah, Wyoming
Southern New England: Connecticut, Massachusetts, Rhode Island
Southwest: New Mexico, Oklahoma, Texas
U.S. Territories and Possessions
Upper Plains: Montana, North Dakota, South Dakota
The West: Arizona, California, Nevada
Western Great Lakes: Illinois, Minnesota, Wisconsin

Florida at a Glance

Area: 65,758 sq mi (170,312 sq km)[1].
22nd-largest state
  Land: 53,625 sq mi (138,888 sq km)
  Water: 12,133 sq mi (31,424 sq km)
Highest elevation: Britton Hill,
  345 feet (105 m)
Lowest elevation: sea level (Atlantic
  Ocean)

Statehood: March 3, 1845 (27th state)
Capital: Tallahassee

Population: 19,893,297
  (third-largest state)[2]

State nickname: Sunshine State
State bird: mockingbird
State flower: orange blossom

[1] *U.S. Census Bureau*
[2] *U.S. Census Bureau, 2014 estimate*

Florida

Historians call the United States a nation of immigrants. Few states reflect that more clearly than Florida. The country's oldest European city—St. Augustine, established by Spanish explorers in 1565—is in the Sunshine State. In modern times, Florida has attracted millions of new immigrants. Some 20 percent of Floridians speak Spanish. Many others speak languages as diverse as French Creole, French, Portuguese, German, and Vietnamese. Not surprisingly, Florida is known for its rich cultural variety.

Geography

Most of Florida is a peninsula extending into the ocean. It has 1,350 miles (2,172 km) of coastline along the Atlantic to the east and the Gulf of Mexico to the west. Although slender, it is one of the country's longest (447 miles [719 km] north to south) and widest (361 miles [581 km] east to west) states because of its unusual shape. Its 65,758 square miles (170,312 square kilometers) ranks it 22nd in size among the U.S. states. Florida shares borders with Georgia to the north and Alabama to the north and west.

Florida has hills and mountains in the north but overall the state is relatively flat. Britton Hill, its highest point, is only 345 feet (105 meters) above sea level. Every other U.S. state has a higher elevation. Florida is mostly green year-round. Many Floridians take trips to Georgia and the Carolinas to enjoy autumn colors.

Major rivers are the St. Johns, St.

Words to Understand in This Chapter

aerospace industry—factories that produce vehicles for space flight and their parts and related businesses.

cede—to turn over a territory to another controlling power.

civil case—a court case that involves charges of individual rights violations.

criminal case—a court case that involves charges of criminal law violations.

high-tech—relating to sophisticated technology, such as electronics and computer science.

immigrant—person who arrives in a country to establish a new residence.

investor—someone who buys something with the hope of selling it later for a profit.

land speculation—buying cheap property, expecting it to increase in value.

New World—the term early European explorers and settlers had for the Americas.

panhandle—the narrow western extension of Florida.

peninsula—a fingerlike part of coastal land projecting into the water.

phosphate—a chemical compound used in fertilizers, carbonated drinks, and many other products.

service sector—industries and businesses that provide services, ranging from lodging to food preparation.

sinkhole—a cavity in the earth's surface; it may be covered by deep layers of surface soil before eventually collapsing.

subtropical—a warm southern region with year-round mild weather, as in most of Florida.

tropical—a warm, frost-free climate, typical of regions near the equator.

South Beach, east of Miami, draws millions of tourists from all over the world. It is known for its nightclubs, restaurants, boutiques, and hotels.

The historic Key West lighthouse, built in 1848, is now operated as a museum that is open to the public.

Marys, Suwannee, Perdido, and Apalachicola. The largest lakes are George in northern Florida and Okeechobee in the northern part of the Everglades. Lake Okeechobee encompasses approximately 700 square miles (1,813 sq km). It is the second-largest freshwater lake in the United States, after Lake Michigan.

Kingsley Lake is a fascinating body of water in north-central Florida. Airline pilots call it Silver Dollar Lake because it is almost perfectly round. The ancient lake is thought to have been formed by a vast sinkhole.

Florida features numerous mineral springs. Throughout history, people have claimed that these springs have healing qualities. Some of Florida's waters are so clear that the bottoms can be observed at depths greater than 50 feet (15 m).

The Everglades is a large area of tropical wetlands in southern Florida.

Tree species are varied: palm, pine, ash, sweet gum, mangrove, hickory, magnolia, and oak, to name only a few. The state also is rich in flowers, such as azalea, dogwood, hibiscus, iris, lily, orchid, bougainvillea, sunflower, camellia, and poinsettia.

Florida's most well-known wild animal is the alligator. In recent decades, the building of houses in wild areas has resulted in news-making encounters between gators and humans. Deer and fox are common. Also seen are black bears, wildcats, and smaller animals, including squirrels, otters, and opossums.

Birds flourish, especially in watery regions. These include heron, egret, pelican, and anhinga colonies. More fish species may exist in and around Florida than anywhere else on the planet. Freshwater fish include bass, catfish, bream, and crappie. The surrounding seas support fish of all sizes, from marlin and tarpon to sea trout and red snapper. Shellfish also abound here.

The state's prominent natural attraction is the Everglades. It is one

Did You Know?

Florida is a very popular state among saltwater scuba and snorkel divers. One of the most visited dive sites in the world is the wreck of the freighter *Benwood*. It lies in shallow waters in the Florida Keys and is home to a colorful assortment of sea creatures. The *Benwood*'s sinking during World War II is a mystery. It collided with another ship, but some historians believe it first was struck by a torpedo.

of the most scientifically studied swamplands in the world. Everglades National Park covers 1.5 million acres (607,028 ha)—and the park is only a fifth of the broader Everglades wetlands.

Florida's climate is subtropical in the northern and central sections, tropical in the south. Icy conditions and snowfall are uncommon. Although Florida is known for its warm climate, temperatures rarely exceed 100° Fahrenheit (38° Celsius). Its record high temperature is 109°F (43°C), recorded in 1931. Its record low, –2°F

A man walks through a Miami street that flooded after Hurricane Sandy hit the city in 2012.

Every March, more than half a million motorcyclists from all over the United States converge on Daytona Beach for "Bike Week." The festivities include motorcycle races and street parties.

Cinderella's Castle is a major attraction at Disney World's Magic Kingdom in Orlando. The popular theme park is the world's most visited, attracting 17 million visitors a year.

Castillo de San Marcos was built to defend St. Augustine, the first Spanish settlement in North America, which was established in 1565.

(–19°C), occurred in 1899. An "extreme weather event" occurred on January 19, 1977, when snow fell on Miami Beach.

Hurricanes are an annual worry for Floridians. According to the National Hurricane Center, more hurricanes have struck Florida than any other East Coast or Gulf Coast state. Since 1851, Florida has been hit by more than 400 storms—almost twice as many as Texas, the next most vulnerable state. They included 35 major hurricanes. A storm in 1928 killed almost 2,000 people. Hurricane Andrew in 1992 caused $23 billion in damage.

History

Evidence from burial mounds suggests that Indians inhabited Florida at least 10,000 years ago. Members of different tribes were hunters, farmers, and fishers.

The Atlantic Coast of what is now

The Tampa Bay area, which includes the cities of Tampa (pictured), St. Petersburg, and Clearwater, is home to more than 2.9 million people.

Florida was one of the first parts of the New World that Europeans explored and settled. Juan Ponce de León landed here first in 1513. He claimed the land for Spain. St. Augustine is the oldest European city in North America. It was established by Spaniards in 1565.

Ponce de León

Two centuries later, in 1763, Spain ceded the territory to England—but British control lasted only 20 years. When the British withdrew from the colonies at the end of the American Revolution in 1783, Florida again became a Spanish domain. Spain surrendered the peninsula to the United States in 1819. Florida became a U.S. territory two years later and a state in 1845.

With the spread of European settlements, conflicts with the Indians made for a violent chapter in Florida's history. After the Second Seminole War (1835–1842), most of the Seminoles were relocated to the Midwest. Their chief, Osceola, was captured and died in prison.

More families began carving out farms during the mid-1800s. The great majority owned relatively small plots of land and no slaves. However, Florida officially was a slave state when it was admitted to the Union. It joined the Confederacy during the Civil War (1861–1865).

The state experienced further population growth in the 1880s. Investors were attracted by the discovery of large deposits of phosphate, used in making countless consumer products. To this day, Florida leads the nation in phosphate production.

By 1896, America's network of rail lines along the Eastern Seaboard had spread all the way to Miami. Engineers began draining swampland in the early 1900s. This created new farmland as well as coastal resort properties. Land speculation in the 1920s boosted the state's population. Many more new residents came after World War II.

Construction began on the Cape Canaveral rocket launch site in 1950. The first rocket was launched that year and the first satellite in 1958. The expanding U.S. space program had a tremendous impact on Florida's economy during the 1960s and 1970s.

Florida's population increased dramatically in the latter half of the 20th century. The communist takeover of Cuba brought almost a million refugees to the state beginning in the 1960s. Further growth spurts occurred in the 1970s and 1980s. New industries and tourism, meanwhile, created thousands of new jobs.

Besides the yearly threat of hurricanes, nature has impacted Florida's history in many ways. Most recently, crop disease and severe freezes destroyed much of the state's citrus production in the 1980s. Wildfires in 1998 devastated broad swaths of land. Preserving the Everglades, which is vital to the ecology, has become a significant challenge.

Government

Since adopting its first constitution in 1838, Florida has had six of them. It ratified its current constitution in 1968. In Washington, the state is rep-

The space shuttle Atlantis *launched from NASA's Kennedy Space Center in Cape Canaveral, July 8, 2011. This was the final flight of the American space shuttle program.*

Florida's current capitol building in Tallahassee, a 25-story tower built during the 1970s, is pictured behind the state's historic capitol, which is now open to the public as a museum.

resented by two U.S. senators and 27 members of Congress.

Five elected officials comprise the executive branch of state government. The governor and lieutenant governor campaign as running mates. Also elected are the three state cabinet heads: attorney general, chief financial officer, and agriculture commissioner. Each official serves a four-year term and may be elected to two terms. Florida's state government structure is noted for the strong powers given to cabinet officers. More than 20 departments and agencies come under the direction of the governor and cabinet heads.

In the legislative branch, the state Senate consists of 40 members, each elected to a four-year term. The 120 members of the House of Representatives are elected to two-year terms. No state legislator can serve longer than eight years. As in other states, the main role of the legislative bodies is to make and revise Florida laws.

Florida's judicial branch consists of the state Supreme Court, five district courts of appeal in different areas of the state, 20 circuit courts, and county courts in each of Florida's 67 counties. Criminal and civil cases are taken up in circuit courts, lesser matters in county courts.

Counties, cities, and towns, plus school districts and special districts, govern local affairs. Special districts oversee airports and other transportation systems, hospitals, beach preservation, water and sewer services, planning/zoning, and other services.

Because of its high population, Florida has 29 electoral votes, far more than any other southeastern state. It is tied with New York and second only to California (55 electoral votes).

The Economy

Florida's economy is impacted greatly by international trade, tourism, and the aerospace industry.

Almost half of the country's exports to South and Central America are channeled through Florida. Not surprisingly, considering its "Sunshine State" recreational attractions,

Did You Know?

The Kennedy Space Center, situated midway along Florida's coastline, has been the site of space launches since the 1960s. Surprisingly, the location was selected despite being in a weather zone of frequent electrical storms—not to mention being on the "hurricane coast." Some launches have been postponed repeatedly because of bad weather. An Apollo moon flight in 1969 actually was struck by lightning during launch but was able to continue its mission.

tourism brings more than $60 billion into the state each year. The economic impact of the space industry is much less than it was during the late 20th century, before the space shuttle program ended, but it remains significant.

Agriculture, the historic base of the state's economy, still flourishes. Florida not only accounts for two-thirds of America's orange supply; it provides approximately 40 percent of orange juice to consumers globally.

Famous People of Florida

Osceola (1804–1838) was a leader of the Seminole people. He resisted the government relocation of his tribe from Florida during America's period of westward expansion.

James Weldon Johnson (1871–1938) is most famous for his leadership roles with the National Association for the Advancement of Colored People (NAACP). But Johnson was a man of many gifts and skills: lawyer, diplomat, university professor, and translator. He was also a novelist, poet, and composer.

James Weldon Johnson

Janet Reno (b. 1938) served as U.S. attorney general during the administration of President Bill Clinton.

John Ellis "Jeb" Bush (b. 1953), son of President George H. W. Bush and brother of President George W. Bush, relocated from Texas to Florida in 1981. He served two terms as Florida's governor, and in 2015 announced his presidential candidacy.

Norman Thargard (b. 1943) has been called "America's first cosmonaut." The meaning is humorous. Thargard was the first American astronaut to serve aboard a Russian spacecraft. (Russian space crews are called cosmonauts.) He was a member of a 1995 Russian/American mission supporting the Russian space station *Mir*.

Among countless sports greats from Florida is Steve "Lefty" Carlton (b. 1944), a Baseball Hall of Famer and winner of four Cy Young Awards. Fort Myers native Deion "Prime Time" Sanders (b. 1967) is the only athlete to play in both a Super Bowl and a World Series. He was elected to the Pro Football Hall of Fame in 2011.

Deion Sanders

Musical talent is wonderfully mixed in the Sunshine State. One of the best-recognized contemporary Florida pop musicians is Howie Durough (b. 1973), a founding member of the Backstreet Boys.

Florida film stars include Faye Dunaway (b. 1941), Burt Reynolds (b. 1936), and Sidney Poitier (b. 1927).

The state is known for producing other citrus fruits—grapefruit, tangerines, limes—as well as vegetables, particularly tomatoes.

Fishing is crucial to Florida's economy. Large catfish are caught in fresh waters. Along the coasts, shellfish, especially shrimp, are staple harvests for commercial fishers. Many seafood items offered on restaurant menus come from Florida's coasts.

Other economic strengths in Florida include the service industry, notably high-tech companies, many of them small ventures, and financial institutions. The construction industry is constantly busy. Health technology projects and university-related research are ongoing.

The People

The U.S. Census Bureau tabulated Florida's population at 18,801,310 in 2010. As of 2014, it was estimated to have grown by about 750,000. That year, the Census Bureau reported that Florida had surpassed New York to claim third place in terms of population, behind only California and Texas.

Chief Osceola and his horse, Renegade, prepare to throw the flaming spear which signifies the start of a Florida State University Seminoles home football game in Tallahassee. While some sports teams have drawn criticism for using names or images that are considered derogatory toward Native Americans, the university has worked closely with the Seminole Nation, and in turn the tribe has historically supported the school and its Seminole mascot.

Many outsiders think of Florida as the country's prime retirement destination and expect most citizens to be in their senior years. Interestingly, while the percentage of Florida's seniors is higher than the national average, only 18.7 percent are 65 and older. By contrast, 20.6 percent are under 18.

The state is heavily traveled by residents and by millions of visitors who come each year. Evidence of its busyness: Florida has more than 800 airports, counting private airfields, seaplane bases, and heliports.

Racially, 78.1 percent of Floridians are white, 16.7 percent black or African American. Hispanics and Latinos (who may be of any race, the Census Bureau explains) represent 23.6 percent of the population.

Floridians age 25 or older who have high school or higher education levels total 85.8 percent, slightly above the national average. About 26 percent hold bachelor's degrees or higher. A language other than English is spoken in 27.3 percent of the homes.

The median household income was $47,309 between 2008 and 2012. During that period, 15.6 percent were below the poverty level; the national average was 14.9 percent.

Major Cities

Tallahassee, in northern Florida near the Georgia border, is the state capital and the Leon County seat. Historically, it has been a farming hub. Today it also is a manufacturing center. Industries produce wood and building materials, processed foods, and many other goods. Educational institutions include Florida State University and the National High Magnetic Field Laboratory, a noted research facility.

Although it's the capital, Tallahassee (population 182,965) is only the seventh-largest city and the center of the 13th-largest metropolitan area in Florida. By far, the heaviest concentration of people live in the southern tip of the peninsula. This metro area encompasses *Miami* (408,750), *Fort Lauderdale* (168,528), *Pompano Beach* (101,617), and neighboring

Jacksonville, the state's largest city, is located on the St. Johns River in northeastern Florida.

municipalities. It is the nation's fourth-largest urban area.

Miami, seat of Miami-Dade County, has a thriving commercial sector, with numerous firms offering financial services and handling world trade. It is constantly alive with cultural and entertainment activity as well. The city's population is mostly Hispanic or Latino, according to the 2010 census. More than a third have a Cuban heritage. Another fifth have South and Central American origins.

Tampa (population 346,037), *St. Petersburg* (244,997), and *Clearwater* (107,784) comprise the state's second-most-populated metro area. Tampa, the central city, is the

Hillsborough County seat. The area is an important industrial and commercial center as well as a prominent Gulf Coast seaport.

Orlando (population 243,195) and surrounding cities and suburbs in central Florida form the third-largest population district. Until the 1970s, this area was primarily a citrus farming center. The opening of Walt Disney World in 1971 touched off an economic shift that resulted in Orlando becoming the most popular amusement park destination in the country. Aerospace and high-tech companies also are vital to the area economy.

Jacksonville (population 827,908), on the northeast coast, is Florida's most populous city, though the overall metro area ranks fourth in the state. It is a major insurance and financial center. The city is named after Andrew Jackson, the first territorial governor and later a U.S. president. (Interestingly, historians believe Jackson never visited Jacksonville.)

Gainesville (population 124,354) is the home of the University of Florida and noted history and art museums. Cities along the Florida panhandle are smaller. *Pensacola* (51,923) has long been important for its naval installations. *Panama City* (36,484) is a popular beach destination. It also is a deepwater port.

Further Reading

Allman, T. D. *Finding Florida: The True History of the Sunshine State*. New York: Atlantic Monthly Press, 2013.

Gannon, Michael, ed. *The History of Florida*. Gainesville: University Press of Florida, 2013.

Hunt, Bruce. *Visiting Small-Town Florida*. Sarasota, FL: Pineapple Press, 2011.

Internet Resources

www.myflorida.com

> This Internet portal offers links to federal, state, and local government offices. It also provides links to consumer information, statistics, and other resources.

www.stateofflorida.com

> An independent Web site that provides state information and links to further information about Florida at other Internet locations.

www.visitflorida.com

> Visit Florida is a guide to tourist destinations in the state.

www.floridahumanities.org

> The Florida Humanities Council is a state-sponsored organization. Its website posts information to help visitors "explore the heritage, traditions, and stories of our state and its place in the world."

Text-Dependent Questions

1. What hurricane devastated the Miami area in 1992, causing $23 billion in damage?
2. In what city is the University of Florida located? Florida State University?
3. How many airports does Florida have?
4. How many representatives does Florida send to the U.S. Congress?

Research Project

Catalog the variety of mammal, reptile, bird, and fish species inhabiting the Everglades. What threatens their habitat?

Georgia at a Glance

Area: 59,425 sq miles (153,910 sq km). 24th largest state[1]
  Land: 57,513 sq mi (148,958 sq km)
  Water: 1,912 sq mi (4,952 sq km)
Highest elevation: Brasstown Bald, 4,784 feet (1,458 m)
Lowest elevation: Atlantic Ocean, sea level

Statehood: January 2, 1788 (4th state)
Capital: Atlanta

Population: 10,097,343 (eighth largest state)[2]

State nickname: Peach State
State bird: brown thrasher
State flower: Cherokee rose

[1] *U.S. Geological Survey*
[2] *U.S. Census Bureau, 2014 estimate*

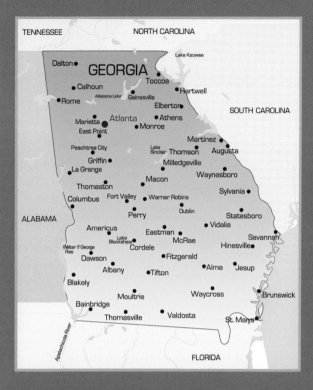

Georgia

Georgia has come a long way since its founding as one of America's 13 colonies. The English king intended it as a great land buffer between the Carolinas and the Spanish and French threats in Florida and to the west. Georgia was settled largely by poor English families, hoping to carve out new lives in the wilderness. Many were imprisoned debtors who had been released and deported to the New World.

The state's rural economy of the 19th and 20th centuries was driven by cotton, rice, indigo, and textiles. Farming remains a mainstay of Georgia's economy. But Georgia has emerged in the 21st century as one of the nation's leading economic centers. It is home to the busiest airport on the planet. Here, you will find one of America's most varied assortments of businesses and industries.

Geography

Georgia is the 24th-largest state in the United States and one of the largest east of the Mississippi River, encompassing 59,425 square miles (153,910 sq km). It is surrounded by five other states: Florida to the south, Alabama to the west, Tennessee and

North Carolina to the north, and South Carolina to the east. At its southeastern corner is a 100-mile (160-km) Atlantic coastline.

Six primary land regions shape the geography of Georgia. The Blue Ridge

---

Words to Understand in This Chapter

aviation industry—factories that make airplanes and airplane parts.

biotechnology—the science of making living organisms into commercial products.

boll weevil—a species of beetle that ravaged Southern cotton crops in the 1920s.

deport—to force a person or group to leave a country.

fuller's earth—a claylike substance used in making absorbents and other products.

House of Commons—the British legislative body consisting of elected, rather than crown-appointed, representatives.

hydroelectric—referring to producing electricity by controlling the flow of rivers.

indigo—a plant that produces blue dye.

kaolin—a form of white clay used in the manufacture of products such as paint and paper.

mound builders—ancient American Indians noted for constructing temple mounds, some of which still can be seen.

philanthropist—one who devotes money and influence to supporting the underprivileged.

revenue—business profits that can be taxed by a local, state, or federal government.

sharecropper—a worker who tended a portion of a landowner's large farm for a share of the profit.

synthetics—products, such as plastics, made from artificial ingredients, rather than from natural substances.

tenant farmer—a worker who rented living quarters on a large farm and paid rent to the landowner from produce sales.

textiles—products made from knitted or woven cloth.

veto—an executive's overriding of a legislature's vote.

The Tallulah River runs past rocky cliffs that rise up to 1,000 feet (300 m) high. A two-mile-long stretch known as Tallulah Gorge has several spectacular waterfalls and is a popular destination for tourists.

Cherry trees bloom in Dunlap Park on a spring evening in Macon.

Kayakers navigate the rapids on the Chattooga Wild and Scenic River. This river runs for 57 miles (92 km), and forms part of the Georgia-South Carolina border.

A mature pecan grove in south Georgia during springtime. Since the late 1800s, Georgia has been the nation's leading producer of pecans.

in the northeast features mountains that rise to almost 5,000 feet (1,524 m). Rivers that form there are vital for generating hydroelectric power. Beautiful waterfalls draw sightseers to the area.

The Appalachian Ridge and Valley region and the Appalachian Plateau are in the northwestern part of the state. Forested ridges are separated by lush valleys. The sandy soil is not very fertile in the plateau region. In the broader valleys farther south, the soil is rich and excellent for farming.

The Piedmont is a zone of rolling hills extending from the Appalachian region to the center of the state. The southern half of Georgia is part of the Atlantic Coastal Plain and the East Gulf Coastal Plain. These are massive lowland regions that extend from Central America to New England.

Many rivers and streams of the north Georgia mountains flow to the Atlantic and Gulf Coasts. Others drain into the Tennessee River, part of the system that empties into the Mississippi. Major rivers are the Savannah, which marks the state's

Did You Know?

"Georgia on My Mind," the state song, became a Billboard No. 1 hit after it was recorded by Ray Charles in 1960. It later was a chart topper when it was covered by country singer Willie Nelson. The light jazz ballad was composed in 1930 by Hoagy Carmichael and Stuart Gorrell.

border with South Carolina, and the Chattahoochee, Altamaha, and Flint. Some of the rivers have been dammed for hydroelectric power production, forming scenic lakes. Georgia lakes include Allatoona, Sinclair, Sidney Lanier, and Seminole. On the Savannah River, Georgia shares two border lakes with South Carolina: Hartwell and J. Strom Thurmond.

Georgia has a generally mild climate, though the northern hills and mountains experience cold winters. The average temperature statewide is about 65°F (18°C). The record high of 113°F (45°C) was reached in 1978. The low of –17°F (–27°C) occurred in

1940. Georgia receives approximately 50 inches (127 cm) of rain and one inch (2.5 cm) of snow annually.

Most of Georgia is woodland—mainly pines and hardwoods in the north, pines and live oaks in the south. Flowers include laurels, daisies, violets, rhododendrons, and roses. Wild animals are abundant: deer, foxes, bears, and smaller animals. Hundreds of bird species include songbirds and game birds. The Okefenokee Swamp in southeastern Georgia is a major bird refuge. Bream, bass, catfish, rainbow trout, eels, and other fish teem in the rivers and lakes. Shellfish thrive in the state's coastal waters.

History

Indians inhabited what is now Georgia more than 10,000 years ago. Some of the earliest people were of the

An American alligator swims past bald cypress trees in the Okefenokee Swamp Wildlife Refuge.

Mississippian culture, known as mound builders. At the time of European settlement, the largest tribes were the Cherokee in the northern region and the Creek in the south. They were vulnerable to contagious European diseases. Smallpox, diphtheria, and measles wiped out much of the native population.

Hernando de Soto led a Spanish expedition through the area in 1540. Almost 200 years passed before the first permanent European settlement was made. James Oglethorpe, a British philanthropist and a member of the House of Commons, persuaded King George II to create a colony here. Oglethorpe wanted to give imprisoned debtors in England a chance for a new life in America. He established a settlement in what is now Savannah. Settlers from Germany and other European countries began immigrating to Georgia to escape religious persecution.

British forces occupied most of Georgia during the Revolution. They withdrew in 1782, and the war ended the next year. Georgia became a U.S. state in 1788. New settlers began arriving in the region in greater numbers during the 19th century.

During the American Revolution, the British Army captured Savannah in 1778. An American attempt to retake the city in 1779 failed, and the British controlled the seaport until the war was nearly over.

So did land grabbers. Shady speculators bribed Georgia politicians to let them buy state land cheaply so they could sell it at a high profit. The controversy, called the Yazoo Fraud, was not settled until 1810.

During the early 1800s, the Creek Indians sold their lands to the state and relocated to the Arkansas Territory. In northern Georgia, many Cherokee wanted to remain. The U.S. Army rounded up the last of the Cherokee and marched them almost a thousand miles to what is now Oklahoma. The forced marches in 1838 and 1839 are remembered as the Trail of Tears.

A slave state, Georgia was part of the Confederacy during the Civil War. Several major battles were fought in northern Georgia, notably at Chickamauga. In September 1864,

Gen. William Tecumseh Sherman's Union army captured Atlanta. They burned the city two months later, then began their destructive "March to the Sea" and northward through the Carolinas. That effectively broke the Confederacy. Confederate commander Robert E. Lee surrendered in April 1865.

Atlanta became the state capital in 1868.

Cotton remained Georgia's most important farm crop after the Civil War and into the 1900s. Most cotton farmers, though, did not own their farms. Rural landowners divided property into small farms that were worked by sharecroppers and tenant farmers. These workers received only part of the money earned from the sale of their crops. The rest went to the landowners.

The Great Depression caused long-term hardship in Georgia, as it did elsewhere. The state weathered other economic woes during the first half of the 20th century. Agriculture, in particular, was ravaged by a boll weevil invasion and drought.

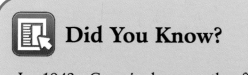

Did You Know?

In 1943, Georgia became the first state to allow 18-year-olds to vote.

This painting shows Union and Confederate troops fighting for Atlanta in 1864. The victory by a Union army commanded by William T. Sherman was a major blow to the Confederacy. Sherman then marched his men through Georgia, plundering farms along the way, until they reached the seaport at Savannah in December 1864.

A family of African-American sharecroppers cultivates a cotton field near White Plains, circa 1941. After the Civil War, many former slaves as well as poor whites who did not own their own farmland became sharecroppers. They would receive the right to farm a piece of land, and at harvest time would give a portion of their crop to the landowner.

Did You Know?

Hartsfield-Jackson International Airport in Atlanta is the world's busiest airport, both in the number of passengers and the number of incoming and outgoing flights. More than a quarter of a million travelers use the airport each day. The facility handles approximately a million flights annually. It has more than 200 arrival and departure gates for passengers.

Good news came from an unexpected economic sector. Two major airlines, Delta and Eastern, established their headquarters at the Atlanta airport. The area became a center of the aviation industry. Other new industries put down roots in different parts of Georgia after World War II. By the end of the 20th century, many prominent national and international companies were based in the Atlanta area.

Like many states, Georgia struggled with the civil rights movement and integration in the 1960s. In 1965, Julian Bond, a black civil rights leader, was elected to the state House of Representatives. Other members of the chamber refused to seat him. The U.S. Supreme Court ruled in Bond's favor in 1966.

In recent years, racial tensions have eased. Georgia has become one of the nation's fastest-growing states with a wide assortment of successful industries and businesses.

Government

Georgia has had many state constitutions since becoming a state. Its current constitution was adopted in 1983. Georgia sends two U.S. senators and 14 congressional representatives to Washington. In presidential elections, the state has 16 electoral votes.

Like the federal government, Georgia's state government consists of executive, legislative, and judicial branches.

The governor and lieutenant governor head the executive branch. Both officials are elected to four-year terms. The governor makes policy decisions, signs or vetoes new laws, appoints agency heads and other state government officials, and has a major influence on the state budget. The lieutenant governor presides over the state Senate and becomes governor if the current governor dies or leaves office. The governor may run for one additional term; the lieutenant governor can serve indefinitely, if reelected.

Other officials elected to the executive branch are the secretary of state, the attorney general, the agriculture commissioner, school superintendent, the labor commissioner, and the commissioner of insurance and fire safety.

The state legislature consists of a 56-member Senate and a 180-member House of Representatives. Legislators are elected to two-year terms and can seek reelection indefinitely. They propose and debate new state laws.

The judicial branch is the court sys-

The Georgia State Capitol building in Atlanta was built in 1889.

tem. The different levels of the court system range from municipal courts, which hear traffic cases and city violations, to state and superior courts, which handle civil and criminal cases. If they lose, parties in those cases can appeal to the state Court of Appeals and ultimately the Georgia Supreme Court.

Georgia's counties, cities, and towns have their own local government structures. Separate powers are given to public school systems and to airport and transit authorities.

The Economy

Most of the income produced in Georgia is through the service sector. Wholesale operations (notably involving food, transportation equipment, and oil products) and retail ventures (such as supermarkets, discount stores, restaurants, and auto dealerships) generate the most revenue. Other important services include hospitals and medical offices, legal and accounting firms, technology companies and stores, and finance and insurance firms.

Georgia's leading farm products are broiler chickens, cattle, eggs, cotton, and peanuts. Peanuts, soybeans, and other crops thrive in the rich soil of southwestern Georgia. Throughout the Atlantic Coastal Plain in the southeast, farmers have large yields of peanuts, onions, watermelons, sweet potatoes, and tobacco. Georgia is the country's top peanut and pecan producer.

Industry is vital to Georgia's economy. Besides the traditional nickname of the "Peach State," Georgians like to call their state the "Empire State of the South." Numerous manufacturers turn raw goods into marketable products. These include processed foods and drinks, textiles, and synthetics. Georgia is a leading state in producing auto and aircraft parts.

Mining also contributes to the state's economy. Georgia produces large quantities of granite, limestone, marble, building stone, and gravel. It leads in the production of fuller's earth and kaolin.

Its location makes Atlanta a major transportation center of the eastern

United States. Atlanta also is a vital rail hub.

Tourism is important in Georgia, as it is in other southeastern states. The state Department of Economic Development calculates that tourism brings some $54 billion annually into the state.

In employee numbers, Georgia's largest employers are military installations, including Fort Benning and Robins Air Force Base.

The People

Georgia's population was 9,687,653, according to the 2010 U.S. census. The Census Bureau estimates that the state's population increased to over 10 million in 2014. Approximately 62.5 percent are white and 31.4 percent black or African American. Some 9.2 percent are Hispanic or Latino (who may identify themselves with any race). Almost 25 percent are under age 18, while 12 percent are age 65

In 1886, an Atlanta pharmacist named Dr. John Pemberton created a soft drink that could be sold at soda fountains. By the 1890s the drink, Coca-Cola, was being bottled and sold throughout the South. Today, Coke products are sold in more than 200 countries worldwide, and consumers drink more than 1.8 billion servings of Coke products a day. The company has maintained strong ties to Georgia, with its world headquarters located in Atlanta.

Famous People from Georgia

Many national leaders were born in Georgia. James E. "Jimmy" Carter Jr. (b. 1924) of Plains was elected president of the United States in 1976. Clarence Thomas (b. 1948) is a U.S. Supreme Court justice. Dr. Martin Luther King Jr. (1929–1968) is the best-known leader of the civil rights movement of the 1960s. Dean Rusk (1909–1994) served as U.S. secretary of state.

Jimmy Carter

Famous writers from Georgia include Joel Chandler Harris (1845–1903), Margaret Mitchell (1900–1949), and Erskine Caldwell (1903–1987). Among thousands of noted musicians hailing from the Peach State are Ray Charles (1930–2004), "Little Richard" (b. 1932), Ray Stevens (b. 1939), Amy Grant (b. 1960), and Kanye West (b. 1977). In April 2015, country singer Luke Bryan (b. 1976) received the "Entertainer of the Year" award from the Association of Country Music.

Martin Luther King

Stage and screen stars with roots in Georgia include Oliver Hardy (1892–1957), half of the Laurel and Hardy comedy team; actresses Joanne Woodward (b. 1930), Julia Roberts (b. 1967), and Dakota Fanning (b. 1994); and actor brothers Stacey (b. 1941) and James (b. 1947) Keach.

Among countless Georgia athletes who have excelled in their respective sports are legendary amateur golfer Bobby Jones (1902–1971), baseball stars Ty Cobb (1886–1961) and Jackie Robinson (1919–1972), and football great Jim Brown (b. 1936).

Perhaps Georgia's most notorious historical character was John H. "Doc" Holliday (1851–1887). A frail dentist-turned-gambler, Holliday sided with Wyatt Earp and his brothers in the Gunfight at the O.K. Corral.

Ty Cobb

Jackie Robinson

and older.

The education level of Georgians has increased significantly in the past 20 years. Today, 84.4 percent of citizens age 25 or older have at least a high school education. About 27.8 percent have at least a bachelor's degree, and 10 percent have master's degrees or above. The median household income was $49,604 during the period between 2008 and 2012.

The state Department of Economic Development points out that Georgians are known for their warm hospitality, but they're more than friendly. They're industrious. Business ownership varies widely. African Americans own more than 20 percent of the state's businesses—three times the national average. Women own approximately 31 percent of businesses, which also is above the norm nationally.

Major Cities

Atlanta, the capital of Georgia, has also been called the "capital of the South." The land contained within the city limits is deceptively small. The sprawling Atlanta metropolitan area spreads into 20 north Georgia counties. It encompasses several large, sep-

The fountain at Forsyth Park is a well-known Savannah landmark.

Atlanta is one of the most important cities in the southeastern United States.

arate municipalities, including Sandy Springs, Roswell, Johns Creek, Alpharetta, Marietta, and Smyrna.

Many of America's best-known corporations are based in the Atlanta area. They include Home Depot, United Parcel Service, Coca-Cola, Delta Airlines, NCR Corporation, and the Turner Broadcasting Corporation, which owns the Cable News Network (CNN). Atlanta is home to the U.S. Centers for Disease Control and Prevention and the Weather Channel. It has three major professional sports franchises: the Atlanta Braves (MLB), the Atlanta Falcons (NFL), and the Atlanta Hawks (NBA).

Atlanta's population in the 2010 census was 420,003—more than twice as many people as in any other

Georgia city. The next two cities in number of residents are *Augusta* (population 195,844) and *Columbus* (189,885). Augusta is renowned nationally and internationally as the setting of the Masters, a famous golf tournament held every April. Augusta also has important medical, biotechnology, and military facilities.

Columbus is the home of Aflac Incorporated, a major insurance provider.

Savannah (population 136,286) is perhaps the state's best-known historic destination. Situated at the mouth of the Savannah River near the Atlantic Coast, it is Georgia's oldest city. Dozens of historic sites and gardens

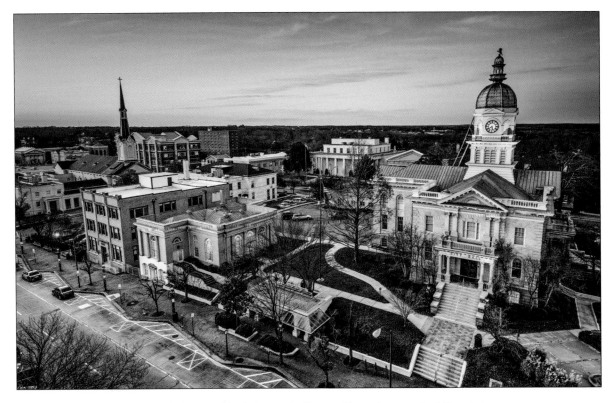

The University of Georgia is located in Athens, in the northeastern part of the state.

are located in and around Savannah. Savannah also is a key seaport.

The University of Georgia is the prominent institution of *Athens* (population 115,452). In fact, the state legislature selected the site in 1801 as the ideal location for a college. UGA is the oldest chartered state university in the United States. After its founding, Athens also became a farming and commercial center. Today, it is one of the state's noted cultural centers. Music and arts organizations are energized by the university.

Macon (population 91,351) is situated in the center of the state. Although the surrounding region is rural, Macon has grown significantly. It is a noted medical, commercial, financial, educational, and cultural center.

Albany (population 77,434) has been the business center of southwestern Georgia almost since its founding in 1836. The Albany Museum of Art contains a significant collection of African art.

Further Reading

Edwards, Leslie. *The Natural Communities of Georgia.* Athens: University of Georgia Press, 2013.

Mcdonald, Janice. *Georgia Off the Beaten Path: A Guide to Unique Places.* Guilford, Conn.: Globe Pequot Press, 2012.

Meyers, Christopher C., and David Williams. *Georgia: A Brief History.* Macon, GA: Mercer University Press, 2012.

 # Research Project

Write a one-page biography of James Edward Oglethorpe, founder of the Georgia colony. What were his achievements? What were his failures?

Internet Resources

www.georgia.org

The Georgia Department of Economic Development provides information about the state's businesses and industries.

www.georgia.gov

This government site contains information about the state—its counties and cities, government agencies, elected officials, and businesses, plus information resources, and more.

http://georgiainfo.galileo.usg.edu

GeorgiaInfo, an online Georgia almanac, publishes a wealth of information online. It is part of the Digital Library of Georgia.

www.metroatlantachamber.com

The Metro Atlanta Chamber of Commerce provides online information about Atlanta area life, education, business, and transportation at this website.

www.georgiaencyclopedia.org

The *New Georgia Encyclopedia* is the first state encyclopedia to be developed exclusively for Internet publication. It was launched in 2004 and is constantly updated. The original 700 articles have been expanded to more than 2,000, covering countless topics.

Text-Dependent Questions

1. How many states share a border with Georgia?
2. In what city do golfers compete in the legendary Masters tournament?
3. What swamp in southeastern Georgia is a major bird refuge?

GREAT SMOKEY MTNS. NATIONAL PARK

NORTH CAROLINA

Spartanburg
Rock Hill
Clemson • Union
Lake Keowee Greenville
Russell Lake Anderson • Laurens
• Greenwood Columbia
SOUTH CAROLINA
• Aiken
Orangeburg
Barnwell
Savannah River Allendale • Walterboro

Bennettsville
Hartsville
Darlington • Florence
Lake City
Sumter Conway • Myrtle Beach
Lake Marion
Lake Moultrie Georgetown

• Charleston

GEORGIA

• Beaufort

ATLANTIC OCEAN

South Carolina at a Glance

Area: 32,020 sq miles (82,931 sq km)[1].
  40th-largest state
  Land: 30,060 sq miles (77,855 sq km)
  Water: 1,960 sq miles (5,076 sq km)
Highest elevation: Sassafras
  Mountain, 3,560 feet (1,085 m)
Lowest elevation: Atlantic Ocean,
  sea level

Statehood: May 23, 1788 (eighth state)
Capital: Columbia

Population: 4,832,482
  (24th-largest state)[2]

State nickname: Palmetto State
State bird: Carolina wren
State flower: yellow jessamine

[1] U.S. Census Bureau
[2] U.S. Census Bureau, 2014 estimate

South Carolina

D r. Walter Edgar, historian and professor at the University of South Carolina, was asked to take on a massive project in 1998. He was to oversee the writing of a complete encyclopedia about his state. It would cover every topic: history, education, government, politics, culture, farming, industry, the arts, and more.

The research, writing, and editing took eight years. Some 600 authors wrote almost 2,000 articles. The hefty reference work contains more than 1,000 pages.

It is little wonder that so much work went into *The South Carolina Encyclopedia*. The state is a rich mix of people and traditions. It has made vital contributions to the United States since the nation was founded.

Geography

South Carolina is one of the smaller states, ranked 40th in size with 32,020 square miles (82,931 sq km). It is bordered by the Atlantic Ocean to the east (187 miles [300 km] of shoreline), North

Carolina to the north and Georgia to the west and south.

South Carolina is spread across an interesting landscape—"from the mountains to the sea," as tourism promoters describe it. The relatively flat Coastal Plain extends about 100 miles (161 km) inland from the coast. It covers roughly half of the state's area. From there, the land rises into sand hills, then fertile, rolling uplands, known as the Piedmont. Looming above, in the northwest corner of the state, are ancient peaks of the Blue Ridge Mountains.

Millions of years ago, geologists

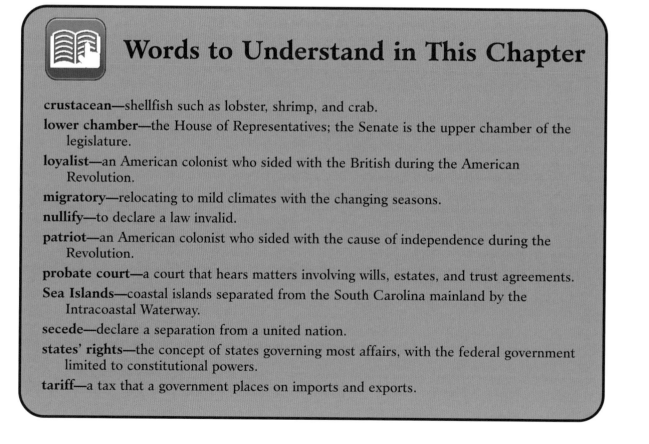

Words to Understand in This Chapter

crustacean—shellfish such as lobster, shrimp, and crab.

lower chamber—the House of Representatives; the Senate is the upper chamber of the legislature.

loyalist—an American colonist who sided with the British during the American Revolution.

migratory—relocating to mild climates with the changing seasons.

nullify—to declare a law invalid.

patriot—an American colonist who sided with the cause of independence during the Revolution.

probate court—a court that hears matters involving wills, estates, and trust agreements.

Sea Islands—coastal islands separated from the South Carolina mainland by the Intracoastal Waterway.

secede—declare a separation from a united nation.

states' rights—the concept of states governing most affairs, with the federal government limited to constitutional powers.

tariff—a tax that a government places on imports and exports.

Reedy River Waterfalls run through the middle of downtown Greenville, South Carolina at Falls Park River Walk.

Azaleas bloom under live oaks and Spanish moss in a South Carolina garden in springtime.

say, what is now the Coastal Plain was under the ocean. Evidence comes from fossils of crustaceans discovered many miles inland.

Population sprawl is what airline visitors first see upon arrival. But South Carolina is actually dominated by forests. Pines are prevalent. Oaks, magnolias, and other hardwoods and softwoods intermingle. The palmetto tree, used for fortress walls and famous for its spongy absorption of cannonballs during the American Revolution, grows along the coast. Common flowers are yellow jessamine, dogwood, azalea, daylily, and mountain laurel.

Animal life is as diverse in South Carolina as it is in most other states. The habitat of white-tailed deer, the state animal, has been shared in recent years by an influx of coyotes.

Scenic view of the Blue Ridge Mountains from Table Rock State Park, near Pickens.

Myrtle Beach is a major tourist destination, attracting about 14 million visitors a year.

Longtime residents include squirrels, chipmunks, rabbits, wild turkeys, red foxes, beavers, and black bears. More than 100 bird species live or spend migratory time in South Carolina. And, of course, there are snakes. Alligators are common in Low Country waters and occasionally are seen in lakes and rivers many miles inland.

Throughout the state are geographic rarities, such as Peachtree Rock, an ancient, gigantic, peachtree-shaped sandstone formation in Lexington County. Forty-Acre Rock, a vast granite slab in Lancaster County, resulted from an ancient volcanic flow. Numerous plant species manage to live atop it, including several endangered species.

Rivers in South Carolina flow from inland—some originating in the Appalachian Mountains—to the sea. Major rivers are the Black, Broad, Congaree, Edisto, Pee Dee, Saluda, and Wateree. The Savannah River forms the border between South Carolina and Georgia.

The state's major lakes are human-made: Marion, Moultrie, Murray, Wateree, Hartwell, and J. Strom Thurmond. They were created with dams to meet industrial and residential needs.

The climate of South Carolina is comparatively warm, though not as mild as Florida's. The average daytime high in summer is about 90°F (32°C). In winter, nighttime lows average around 32°F (0°C). Temperatures are warmer along the coast than in the foothills. The record high temperature, 111°F (43.5°C), occurred in 1954. The record low, –19°F (–28°C), occurred in 1985.

Like Florida, Georgia, and other Atlantic Coast states, South Carolina has weathered many hurricanes. The most destructive in modern times was Hurricane Hugo in 1989. It made landfall in Charleston and caused great damage and power outages far inland. In 1893, an unnamed hurricane killed more than 2,000 people when it ravaged the Sea Islands.

Earthquakes are less frequent but equally scary natural events. The most powerful quake occurred in 1886, centered near Summerville. It was felt throughout the eastern United States and as far away as Canada and the islands of Cuba and Bermuda. It toppled buildings and caused more than $5 million in damage—an enormous sum at that time—in Charleston.

History

More than 30 Indian tribes lived in the region when the first Europeans arrived. The largest were the Cherokee in the northwest, the Catawba to the east, and the Yamasee along the southern coast. Most of them farmed for a living.

Spanish explorers visited what is now South Carolina as early as 1521.

Tourists flock around the Angel Oak Tree in Charleston. The Angel Oak is 66.5 feet (20 m) tall and is estimated to be around 500 years old.

The World War II-era aircraft carrier USS Yorktown *is permanently docked at Patriot's Point Naval and Maritime Museum on the Cooper River in Charleston.*

Sergeant William Jasper raises the flag over Fort Moultrie on June 28, 1776. South Carolina patriots drove off a British fleet to win an early victory in the American Revolution.

Historians date the founding of the state to 1670. In that year, an English expedition established a permanent settlement at Albemarle Point near modern-day Charleston. At first, the two Carolinas were joined as one English province. South Carolina became a separate colony in 1719.

The colony grew in population. More immigrants came from Europe. Earlier settlers moved there from Pennsylvania and Virginia. Most were families who supported themselves on small farms. Others owned large plantations, relying on slave labor. By the time of the Revolutionary War, the colony's population consisted of about 70,000 whites and 100,000 blacks.

Most of the fighting during the Revolution was in the form of local skirmishes between loyalists and patriots. Neighbors often fought against neighbors. Several major battles also occurred here. The patriot victory at Kings Mountain in October 1780 is considered by some historians to have been the turning point in the Revolution. Until then, the Americans had been beaten repeatedly in the southern colonies. The Kings Mountain outcome compelled the British to withdraw from the Carolinas.

South Carolina became the eighth state of the United States in 1788. Two years before, the state legislature, meeting in Charleston, had found a site in the middle of the state to replace Charleston as the capital. They named it Columbia.

South Carolina's reputation as a place with a fiercely independent spirit dates to the 1820s. The state prospered by trading directly with European nations. The federal government imposed heavy tariffs on trade in 1828 and 1832. These tariffs hampered trade. In protest, the state legislature voted to nullify the tariffs, declaring them unconstitutional. President Andrew Jackson—a native South Carolinian—threatened to send troops to enforce the tariffs. Congress headed off a conflict by passing a compromise tariff act.

By 1861, a catastrophic crisis had developed between the northern and southern states. Heated debates and violence centered on the issues of slavery and states' rights. In December 1860, South Carolina became the first of 11 Southern states—called the Confederacy—to secede from the Union. Confederate troops took control of Fort Sumter in Charleston Harbor in April 1861. It was the first significant action of the Civil War.

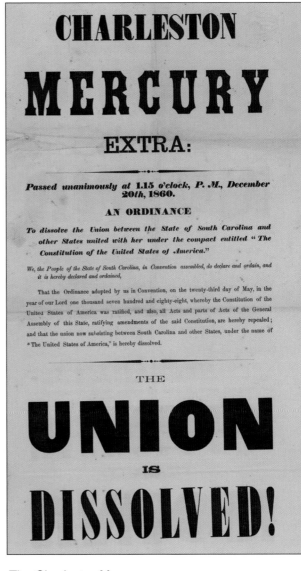

The Charleston Mercury *newspaper announces that South Carolina has voted to secede from the Union, December 1861.*

The first shots of the Civil War were fired at Fort Sumter, located on an island in Charleston Harbor, on April 12, 1861.

Young women operate machinery in a textile mill in Newberry, 1908. After the Civil War, many Southern towns desperate for industry invested in cotton mills. The mills were a central part of life in many South Carolina communities until the 1980s and 1990s, when competition from companies in Asia and the Caribbean, where labor costs were lower, drove many textile mills out of business.

Few major Civil War engagements occurred in South Carolina. Like Atlanta, much of Columbia was burned by Sherman's troops near the end of the war in 1865. And like citizens of other southern states, South Carolinians endured severe hardship as they struggled to rebuild their economy following the South's defeat in the Civil War.

While farms faltered, a new industry provided thousands of jobs. Textile mills paid low wages and required long hours of labor—but at least they paid. The textile industry flourished in South Carolina until the late 20th century.

Farming remained important to the state's economy. Setbacks occurred, particularly with the boll weevil invasion of cotton fields in the 1920s. Many farmers turned to other crops, such as wheat, fruit, and tobacco.

In 1953, the U.S. government began producing nuclear materials at the Savannah River Plant near Aiken. The facility and related industries brought new jobs. Various industries began building factories in other parts of the state. At the same time, major Army, Navy, and Air Force bases bolstered the state's economy. And the state began tapping a rich vein of undeveloped revenue: tourism.

The civil rights movement of the 1950s and 1960s encountered stubborn opposition in South Carolina, both publicly and in state and local governments. But in 1970, three black candidates were elected to the state House of Representatives. They were the first blacks in the lower chamber since 1902. In 1983, the first black since 1888 was elected to the state Senate.

State politics underwent a period of massive change in the 20th century. Until the late 1960s, Democrats held almost all elected offices. In 1974, James B. Edwards was elected the first Republican governor in a century. By the early 2000s, Republicans controlled the state legislature.

South Carolina's economy still depends largely on agriculture. But it also is driven by many industries. Almost 2,000 foreign-owned companies have operations in South Carolina.

The South Carolina State House in Columbia has chambers where the state legislature meets, as well as offices for the governor and lieutenant governor. Construction of the capitol building began before the Civil War, but was not completed until 1907. Today, it is a National Historic Landmark.

This recent surge in economic diversity has changed the complexion of the state. It affects social interaction, arts and culture, education, and other aspects of life in the Palmetto State.

Government

South Carolina government is guided by the state constitution that was adopted in 1895. Since then, the constitution has undergone revisions. The constitution mandates three branches of government.

As in other states, the governor is head of the executive branch. The governor serves a four-year term and may be elected to two consecutive terms. Among other powers, the governor appoints the heads of 15 state agencies, including the State Law Enforcement Division, the Department of Social Services, and the Department of Motor Vehicles.

South Carolinians elect eight other statewide officers to four-year terms: lieutenant governor, attorney general, secretary of state, state treasurer, commissioner of agriculture, superintendent of education, adjutant general, and comptroller general.

The two-chamber legislative branch of state government makes and revises laws. The state Senate has 46 elected members, while the House of Representatives has 124 members. Senators are elected to four-year terms, representatives to two-year terms.

The state Supreme Court is the highest level of the judicial branch. The court's five justices are elected to 10-year terms by members of the state legislature. Sixteen circuit courts throughout the state try criminal and civil cases. Local and special cases are processed in municipal, probate, family, and magistrate courts.

Counties and municipalities have local governments with both elected and appointed officials.

South Carolina is represented in Washington by two U.S. senators and seven members of the House of Representatives. The state casts nine electoral votes in presidential elections.

The Economy

The service sector accounts for the majority of jobs in South Carolina. Workers are employed by government

South Carolina ranks second in the nation (behind California) in producing fresh peaches. It produces about twice the tonnage in peaches as its neighbor Georgia, the "Peach State."

Famous People from South Carolina

The birthplace of Andrew Jackson (1767–1845), seventh president of the United States, has always been disputed by South and North Carolina historians. *The South Carolina Encyclopedia* states that he was born in the Waxhaw settlement of South Carolina.

South Carolina was the scene of more battles and skirmishes during the American Revolution than any other colony. Patriot leaders included Andrew Pickens (1739–1817), a backcountry militia commander, and Francis Marion (1732–1795), a guerrilla leader. Marion was known as the "Swamp Fox" because he hid in Low Country swamplands, difficult for British pursuers to penetrate.

John C. Calhoun (1782–1850) was one of the most important political figures during the first half of the nineteenth century. He served as U.S. secretary of war, secretary of state, and vice president, as well as in both houses of Congress.

John C. Calhoun

Mary McLeod Bethune (1875–1955) was a co-founder of Bethune-Cookman College in Florida. She was also a presidential adviser and civil rights activist.

Bernard Baruch (1870–1965) was a prominent financier. He served as adviser to presidents Woodrow Wilson and Franklin D. Roosevelt.

South Carolina placed many astronauts in NASA's space program. They include Ronald E. McNair (1950–1986), who died when the space shuttle *Challenger* exploded, and Charles M. Duke (b. 1935), the youngest person to walk on the moon.

In sports, South Carolina's most famous athlete is Joseph Jefferson Wofford Jackson (1888–1951), remembered as "Shoeless Joe." He worked in mill rooms as a child, excelled in mill league baseball, and became one of major league baseball's all-time greats. Shoeless Joe Jackson's extraordinary feats on the diamond were tarnished by the Black Sox scandal of 1919. Althea Gibson (1927–2003) was the first African-American tennis player to win at Wimbledon. Joe "Smokin' Joe" Frazier (1944–2011) was a world heavyweight boxing champion.

agencies, health and education entities, retail businesses, banks and other financial services companies, professional services firms, transportation providers, and recreational businesses.

Tourism has become a major source of revenue, especially during the past half century. It brings in some $20 billion a year. Visitors from other states and abroad come for the state's internationally publicized events and attractions and to relax in temperate surroundings rich in history and charm.

Agriculture is important to the state's economy. Until the mid-20th century, South Carolina was mainly an agricultural state. Today, livestock (chickens, beef, turkeys, hogs) and their by-products are leading agricultural products. Corn, cotton, tobacco, peaches, and vegetables go to market from South Carolina farms. Important crops today also include greenhouse and nursery products—from flowers to shrubs. Forestry is a major industry, producing lumber, pulp, and paper.

The coastal fishing industry has been challenged by ecological changes. Still, fishers take valuable catches, especially shrimp.

Leading industrial products include chemicals, textiles, fibers from cloth, and pharmaceuticals.

South Carolina has long been one of the nation's largest *kaolin* producers. Limestone, granite, and other minerals add to the state's economic output.

The People

South Carolina's population grew from 4,625,364 in 2010 to an estimated 4,774,839 in 2013, according to the U.S. Census Bureau. Some 68.3 percent of citizens were white, 27.9 percent black or African American. Hispanics or Latinos (who may identify with different races) comprised 5.3 percent of the population.

South Carolinians under age 18 account for 22.6 percent of the total population while those age 65 and older represent 15.2 percent.

For the period between 2008 and 2012, 84 percent of citizens age 25 and older had at least a high school diploma. Approximately 24.6 percent

A row of historic homes in Charleston's Battery neighborhood.

held bachelor's degrees. The median household income was $44,623.

Major Cities

Named after Christopher Columbus, *Columbia* is the state capital and the Richland County seat. It was the first "planned" state capital in the United States. The site was selected mainly because it is located approximately in the middle of the state. It is also at the juncture of two main rivers, the Broad and Saluda. Today it is an interstate highway hub, where I-20, I-26, and I-77 intersect. Major U.S. highways also pass through and around the city, as do freight and passenger rail lines.

Columbia has the state's largest city population (131,686). For many years, much of its economy has been connected to Fort Jackson, a U.S. Army training base, and the University of South Carolina, a major research institution. Industry, technology, small business, government, and tourism are other leading economic drivers. Besides USC, several other universities, colleges, seminaries, and technical schools are in Columbia. Scores of historic sites, many of them on the National Register of Historic Places, are in the city and throughout Richland County.

An even greater tourist draw is historic *Charleston* (population 125,583), the state's busy international seaport. Horse-drawn carriages take guests along cobblestone streets downtown and along the Battery, the city's famous seawall. Charleston's historic plantation gardens are world-renowned. For decades, Charleston's economy has depended largely on its military installations. The city is home to the Citadel military college and the Medical University of South Carolina. The College of Charleston is America's oldest city college, established in 1770.

The South Carolina upstate along I-85 has become an industrial boom zone. The area has drawn major international companies. They include automotive giants BMW and Michelin, as well as aeronautical and heavy equipment manufacturers.

In the center of it is *Greenville* (population 60,709), one of America's fastest-growing cities. In addition to its business and industry, Greenville is a cultural and entertainment center. Several universities and colleges are situated in and near the city. Its location near the mountains makes it a popular starting point for outdoor adventurers.

Further Reading

Bass, Jack, and W. Scott Poole. *The Palmetto State: The Making of Modern South Carolina.* Columbia: University of South Carolina Press, 2009.

Edgar, Walter, ed. *The South Carolina Encyclopedia.* Columbia: University of South Carolina Press, 2006.

Harmon, Daniel E. *South Carolina Past and Present.* New York: Rosen Central, 2011.

Rogers, Aïda, ed. *State of the Heart: South Carolina Writers on the Places They Love.* Columbia: University of South Carolina Press, 2013.

Text-Dependent Questions

1. What South Carolinian became the first African American to win a tennis championship at Wimbledon?
2. In what year did the great Charleston-Summerville earthquake, which was felt as far away as Canada and the island of Bermuda, occur?
3. What and where is the oldest municipal college in the United States?
4. What river separates South Carolina and Georgia?

Internet Resources

www.scchamber.net

South Carolina Chamber of Commerce website includes a listing of businesses, organized by category, and other business information.

http://scdah.sc.gov

South Carolina Department of Archives and History is a major online source of information about all facets of South Carolina history.

www.scprt.com

The South Carolina Department of Parks, Recreation, and Tourism gateway points to online information at sources including DiscoverSouthCarolina.com, SouthCarolinaParks.com, SCTrails.net, SC-HeritageCorridor.org, and SCFilmOffice.com.

www.scsos.com

Consumer information and links to consumer service sites are included on the Website of the South Carolina Secretary of State.

www.statelibrary.sc.gov

In addition to coordinating the state's public libraries, the South Carolina State Library site contains numerous links to sources of information about South Carolina.

 # Research Project

Learn about the dramatic shifts in South Carolina's economy since the Civil War. What caused the rise and decline of the textile industry? Which farm crops were most important then and now? Why have international industries been attracted to South Carolina in recent decades?

Index

Numbers in **bold italics** refer to captions.

Series Glossary of Key Terms

bicameral—having two legislative chambers (for example, a senate and a house of representatives).

cede—to yield or give up land, usually through a treaty or other formal agreement.

census—an official population count.

constitution—a written document that embodies the rules of a government.

delegation—a group of persons chosen to represent others.

elevation—height above sea level.

legislature—a lawmaking body.

precipitation—rain and snow.

term limit—a legal restriction on how many consecutive terms an office holder may serve.